THE MIDDLE LINE

THE MIDDLE LINE

A different way of doing business!

RONAN FOLEY

Dedicated to Annette, Mia & Siân

"I am absolutely convinced there's a better way of doing business and for me that means delivering both commercially and socially. I believe that a truly sustainable business must recognise and engage with all stakeholders and that, as leaders, we must take individual and collective responsibility for our actions and how we conduct business."

It's About Changing the World

I have spent my life working for corporates and climbing the proverbial career ladder, taking on challenge after challenge by changing, building and ultimately growing businesses successfully.

The last business I turned around was in a challenging position when I was asked to come in as CEO. It had just lost a quarter of its revenue and needed a new strategic direction and vision for the future. The Board and staff had done an exceptional job in shaping the business over the years but it was now in need of new leadership at CEO level and I was delighted to be appointed to the role and set about building on the strong leadership already shown by the Chairman during what were challenging times for the business and sector. In short, it was in my view the perfect role for me.

By the end of my five-year tenure, the Board, staff and wider stakeholder base had delivered €400m profit, €783m in surplus capital, commercial dividends of €55m, €12m in social dividends to society, 28% growth and secured an 'A' rating from ratings agency Standard & Poor's.

So what?! It's just another corporate story, I hear you say. Well, I agree to a certain extent but what I learned and achieved personally was about way more than business success. I believe we fundamentally changed the traditional business model forever and, in doing so, delivered the company's strongest ever set of results, transformed a culture and delivered for communities in a way that had never been done before.

"It's about changing the world from your own doorstep."

Being Good Is Good For Business

Imagine a scenario where it became the norm for businesses around the world that announce an annual commercial dividend to also commit to issuing a social dividend on behalf of society. Imagine if this new norm became intrinsically strategic for all organisations. I believe this vision is the new model for business and that ultimately 'being good is good for business'.

"Being good is good for business and it's ok to say it."

In August 2011, I joined a company in the role of CEO and, from the outset, I painted a picture of a business that would be sensitively reshaped in three significant ways:

1) We will work hard to create the best PLACE to work

2) We will aim for the strongest BUSINESS performance possible

3) We will make a significant DIFFERENCE to society

I coined these three core strands as our 'Place, Business, Difference' or PBD model for business. My belief was that each strand of the model would be interdependent and, when combined, would create a self-perpetuating cycle of renewal.

Greatest Place, Business & Difference

In order to maximise the success of a business it's essential to create the right working environment for your employees.

"Ask yourself whether you want your office environment to reflect 'Downtown Mumbai' or 'Fontainebleau Forest'."

The physical surroundings your team work in and the tools they are given to perform their roles need significant attention, and companies need to invest here first in order to shape things for the future.

Staff will put up with a lot and live with working conditions that can, in some cases, be very poor in terms of basic amenities, e.g., lighting, seating, air quality or desk size.

My advice is to invest in creating vibrant and positive working environments. Make everyone feel appreciated and demonstrate that you care about their surroundings and are willing to make regular improvements.

Trust me, if your employees see this in action it will make for a much stronger sense of positivity throughout your organisation and lead to a greater sense of pride in the company. This doesn't necessarily mean a huge financial investment and can often be something very small in nature.

In a previous role as Managing Director, the staff were surprised one day to find a wall in the office had been painted a deep and luxurious colour red and matching couches had been installed. They thought I'd lost my mind, frankly, but my intention was to create a talking point and to break the monotony of sterile colour. Within a short period, we found that staff were using the area more for conversations over coffee, and it became a real talking point for visitors to the office and a regular location for photo calls. For me, it demonstrated that with a simple tin of paint and a bit of courage you can create a better place for staff and, by doing so, motivate people in some small way.

A week later we introduced head-and-neck massage treatments once a week and, for a relatively small amount of investment, we again improved the working environment and wowed the staff in the process.

Small changes like these can make a significant difference to morale and demonstrate that your company cares. As a result, employees will enjoy their working day more and work better as a result.

When setting the scene in terms of explaining 'Place' to staff, I expressed my absolute conviction at a very early stage that we would, within a three-year period, dramatically improve their working arrangements. This would, in turn create the best possible environment for staff and a platform to produce better business results.

I explained to staff that I wanted to create an atmosphere

both aesthetically and culturally that would instill a sense of excitement, enjoyment, and allow them take pride in their business, office and colleagues. The idea was that this would be a set of improvements which would set us apart from our competitors and create a positive talking point with friends and family.

In choosing our new office location and design, I decided to take a personal interest in the detail around the final location and the design itself. I'd already made a personal commitment to deliver a fantastic 'Place' for staff and I wanted to make sure I got it right. It may appear a bit hands-on for a CEO to get involved in this level of detail but I believed that, of all the key transformational changes we would be making, this was going to be one of the most strategic in nature. It would, I believed, set the future tone, image and profile for the business in the years ahead.

In considering the design of your office, don't make the mistake most other companies make. I recall going through the relocation process in a previous job and, whilst not directly involved, I remember a presentation from the design team where they had completed extensive research into other insurance companies. I couldn't understand why they hadn't broadened their horizons and looked outside of the insurance market at the wider options within other sectors. There was nothing inspirational or remotely different to other insurers and I felt that this was an opportunity missed.

I started looking at companies outside of my own sector, such as technology and social media, and I particularly liked what Skype had done in Amsterdam. I could see that some companies were creating amazingly innovative and award winning new work environments for employees to engage with. One word of warning though: it's important not to create a 'playground' for staff – the environment should be a smart, vibrant and attractive place to feel confident working in.

It's an amazing thing to witness but I believe that when you get this aspect right you will see subtle but important changes to the level of professionalism throughout the office. I recall an instance the first day in our new offices when I noticed a staff member picking up a piece of paper in the corridor and putting it in his pocket. If you can deliver the right 'Place' for staff they will respond and take pride in its appearance and own it, not because they have to but because they want to.

However, simply creating the right canvas doesn't go far enough when you are looking to create the right foundation to build or transform a company for greater future success. A great place to work must also take into account the culture and behaviour of the company and its people.

I recall a story I told the evening we announced our new office location to help position this concept with staff.

The CFO of a company had arranged a meeting with an external auditor to his firm, and his arrival was announced at reception. The CFO greeted the visitor in reception and enquired as to whether he had found a parking space OK. The visitor explained that, after some searching, he found a spot but did notice that there was a car parked illegally in a space specifically for disabled customers or staff. Upon hearing this news, the CFO asked to be shown to the offending car and the auditor duly obliged. He then went to reception with the registration number of the offending car and asked that the individual be contacted and invited to join them in reception. On arrival, the CFO then brought the employee out to the space and explained that this type of behaviour was unacceptable and not in keeping with the principals of the company. The auditor was incredibly impressed that the CFO had taken it upon himself to resolve the matter personally rather than leaving it to someone else.

This form of ownership is gold dust for creating and embedding an engaging and dynamic culture where individuals act responsibly and care about matters beyond what it says in the balance sheet or their job profile.

The following morning when entering our old offices, I noticed that someone had picked up the post from the floor in the hall and someone else had carried the delivery of milk through. I find this type of behavioural change really inspiring as someone in the organisation had that morning decided to change and, as a result, our 'Place' of work had become instantly better.

Building a culture of trust within organisations is another key element to focus on. Employees need to feel trusted by you and it's your responsibility to explore different ways to create a trusting culture.

Here are some practical but small changes you should consider introducing:

Internet access should be available to all staff at any time of the day. So, if a staff member needs to do their shopping or banking online, let them do it without the need to request formal permission or go to a dedicated open computer at certain times of the day. Naturally, there has to be rules and policy guidelines around this but if you learn to trust your employees more and remove some of the old shackles that poison modern businesses, then staff will respect your confidence in them and respect their company more.

Creativity is key to staff morale and your company's success, so it's important you create a platform for creating ideas.

What worked for me was to create an ideas forum where staff could literally suggest changes to any aspect that occurred to them. This strategy, together with quarterly idea sessions with staff, helps build a positive and vibrant culture where staff feel ownership of their own destiny.

There is no need to incentivise this activity because it should come naturally once you've created the right atmosphere and environment in which to do so. However, you must deliver on a large number of these ideas and make sure things change. I call this simple approach "Ideas To Action".

Another important area to get right is building strong leadership. The strength of your business and its future success depends on selecting the strongest leaders. So, if you have a manager in place who was, for example, promoted through the ranks because of experience or technical knowledge rather than ability to lead, you may need to review things. This may seem a bit harsh but I firmly believe that leadership is not something you are taught or learn, but is part of an individual's DNA. All the external courses in the world can help to hone a natural leader's ability but won't make a leader out of someone who quite frankly isn't one!

Be bold but fair with those in leadership roles that clearly aren't up to the task and either move them into a more suitable position or exit them. Do not procrastinate, as it will ultimately negatively impact you, your business and the individual concerned.

"Sometimes even leaders don't know that they can lead."

When I first met Joan, an insurance underwriter, she came across as a very bright and massively capable individual. I had just taken up a new role and I was assessing staff members on an individual basis. However, Joan struck me as someone that had something special, something that made her stand out from the crowd – and this was an ability to lead!

Later that year, I asked Joan to meet me for coffee away from the office and to arrive with a plan for how she might structure and run the department she was currently part of. We met and Joan ran through her plan. It was a good plan but she had carefully avoided making changes to roles and reporting lines where those individuals had, on paper, more technical experience than her or were more senior.

I suggested to Joan that I believed she had the ability to lead the entire department and that she should move into that role. It was amazing to note her response – 'they trained me up', 'they have more experience', 'people would be upset and never stand for such a radical shift in leadership'.

However, we implemented the changes without any problem over the following weeks and Joan was placed in the position of leader. It's amazing what we fear sometimes. 'What will others think?' 'How will they react?' In reality, some people without obvious leadership ability think they should put themselves forward and are encouraged to do so by their companies for all the wrong reasons. However, if you actually take the time to really explain what's expected of the role, you may find that they have no real burning ambition to lead at all!

In short, the technical skills gap that Joan faced was resolved through accelerated training but the fact of the matter was that the leadership trait was there at a relatively junior level and it was important that I recognised it and placed her in a leadership position without delay.

Joan went on to flourish in the role and deliver exceptional results for herself, her team and the business.

Turning Negative People Positive

We've all experienced negative or disruptive individuals who can, if left unaddressed, lead to a slow but fatal osmosis of negativity right the way through your team or business. Believe me when I say that this is a simple situation to address.

In my experience, these individuals are easy to spot and so, once again, be honest about things and start identifying them as a first step. No costly research or analysis should need to be undertaken; just discuss the matter with trusted colleagues and identify the individuals concerned. This, again, may sound crude but it really needs to be a simple process.

The next step is to identify the individuals they have managed to 'infect'. These are the people who you would recognise as being easily influenced and who tend to succumb to a negative view if expressed by a stronger colleague. They often then adopt this perspective in order to 'fit in'.

Once you have gone through this process of identifying, it will be time to speak to the key individual concerned. Try and be as open and honest as possible with the individual and seek their honesty in return, discussing their views and concerns. Often, in my experience, a positive person turns negative when something changes about which they may feel uncomfortable or which is perceived to impact their position or status. What ever it is, it tends to be fundamentally about change and how it impacts 'me'.

Once you've established what concerns the individual has, and this may take a few chats, you need to set your focus on the 'Turn'. There may be things that come up that are pretty easy to address and you should deliver on these immediately. Use the line "and if I was to fix this how would you feel then?"

Some of the suggested grievances might be around recent changes, or the way things should have, in their view, been changed. If any of the suggestions sound good, you then need to ask the individual to take responsibility for this positive change or initiative. Ask them to look into it and come back with a very short proposal, communicate it to staff and move ahead with delivering it.

Staff, familiar with hearing negative thoughts and comments from this individual, should now see a different person, and this will have a transformational and immediately positive impact on their own behaviour and attitudes.

One other area to examine is whether the negative individual might be in the wrong role. It never ceases to amaze me how many organisations put great people into the wrong jobs. I've found that in some cases the individual concerned just needs to be saved and given a fresh or more appropriate function. There is nothing more frustrating for someone than to be in a role that they are fundamentally unsuited to and then expected to do amazing things. So, start rescuing people by either changing aspects of their current role or moving them into a more suitable one.

"Your biggest blockers can become your greatest asset as negative people can turn positive."

Is Cultural Change Easier in a Small Team?

I couldn't begin to count the number of times this comment has been made to me in order to excuse or explain the challenge or complexity of cultural or transformational change in large businesses. I'm sorry but this is complete fallacy!

In my view it shouldn't matter how large an organisation is once you have the right leadership in place at every level. Once you do, cultural change is simple regardless of scale. However, this change must happen simultaneously from the top down and bottom up. A leader can deliver a new perspective and look to change the culture gradually, but it will usually be pointless unless you have a team that can deliver the message.

The first step is to create a clear vision and picture of

what you feel best describes the type of culture you believe in. This cultural vision needs then to be communicated to your employees in both verbal and written form. Draw up a set of values you feel are important to you, e.g., punctuality, trust or openness, and communicate these to all staff.

This may seem a bit different in terms of approach but what worked for me was to host an initial 'Town Hall' session with the entire company to kick things off. I then followed this up with a summary note to all employees introducing myself and re-emphasising what was important to me in terms of shaping the right culture within the organisation. In my initial address and subsequent note to staff I painted a picture of an exciting new direction for the company in terms of culture and gave my commitment to recognising achievements throughout the business.

My aim was to remove some of the mystique a new boss creates when they start a role and build momentum around a new and exciting chapter for the company, one which recognised the past but also helped form a strong sense of excitement or buzz about the future.

You then need to actively deliver on all of this from your own personal perspective and acknowledge when you see others, especially your direct management team, reinforcing or displaying similar values or encouraging others.

To assist this process of renewal, I set about meeting all staff on a one-to-one basis. This may sound time consuming and, in very large organisations near impossible, but I met 150 employees individually within the first few months for at least twenty minutes and it was incredibly beneficial.

Remember, what's important to one individual can be completely different to the next. Take the time to note all the concerns, wishes and ambitions individuals may have about the organisation, their careers and the future challenges or direction of the company. This one-to-one engagement will give you a fantastic insight into the organisation's existing culture, its strengths, talents and weaknesses. It will also demonstrate to staff that as a leader you're listening to everyone and not just a few, and that you are taking all their views seriously.

Once you've completed your one-to-ones, set about

trying to solve, change or facilitate transition by addressing some of those low-hanging fruit on your long list of items. In some cases, it may make sense to ask the individual with the suggestion to take a leadership role in running a project, etc.

It's incredibly important that you set about delivering this list for staff and for them to see that you don't just listen, you act!

Chief Executive Advisory Council

As a CEO you naturally seek the guidance and advice of your Board & Executive Team but it's also important to gain knowledge from others within the business and to look at ways of identifying and nurturing these individuals as much as possible.

One of the key successes for me in terms of shaping a new culture was to create a forum whereby I could engage with staff at all levels in a small group and explore strategic challenges facing the business.

To facilitate this, I launched the Chief Executive Advisory Council (or CEAC), which identified potential future leaders or individuals that stood out in terms of attitude, ability and contribution to the business. With input from my direct management team, I set about introducing the concept to all staff and announcing the first group members.

The CEAC met every quarter for half a day and we discussed some specific strategic challenges facing the business and ran various projects where the team would have to consider the matter in hand, investigate a potential solution and report back at the next meeting. The term set for all members was twelve months to ensure it remained fresh and to recognise different staff annually.

I personally believe the CEAC had a significant impact on shaping the culture and provided me with an amazing opportunity to get new input from staff I wouldn't normally get to hear from. It also recognised talent of all ages and experience within the company and brought those individuals to the fore. It ultimately produced some of the most important improvements for the company, staff and customers within a relatively short period of time.

45 Minutes

Suzanne had just applied for an internal role but wasn't feeling confident about succeeding as she didn't feel she had enough external experience, having spent a large part of her career with just one company. I asked her to consider requesting meetings with market competitors to see what she could learn and to arm herself with new knowledge. I further suggested that she did everything possible to eliminate doubts in her own mind and that of the interviewers that she might not have all the skills necessary for the role.

As part of our brief chat, we also discussed some simple things she could do for herself and with her team to make it a better place to work. I suggested some practical things to try, and plans she could adopt without the need for official clearance from her boss.

Suzanne sent me a note after our 45 minute chat and

here's what she said:

Dear Ronan,

Many thanks for your time on Monday. I found it really helpful. You are a true inspiration. Never has one person inspired and motivated me so much in just 45 minutes. I have already been reflecting on your ideas and challenges and put some of the strategies in place, departmentally and personally. Will let you know how things go.

Separately Paul and I have discussed finding me a mentor, and you were one of a few names he mentioned. I'd very much like to pursue this with you please. Hopefully it would not take too much of your time, if the focus you displayed on Monday is anything to go by!

Look forward to hearing from you,

Sue

I was delighted to receive this note and it was great that Sue took the opportunity to capture this moment in time. Look, there is no magic here! What simply happened was that I listened, questioned, suggested and, above all built a sense of excitement in Sue about her future and her strengths. This in turn got her thinking differently – and much more positively – about how she could shape things. Sue left my office buzzing with ideas and ambition.

My point is that creating a world-class work environment is about taking a genuine interest in others and helping them to achieve things they never thought possible. It is the most satisfying thing I get to do.

Creating a great place to work is, as I mentioned earlier, all about creating the foundation for future business success and bringing staff engagement to a new level. When you get this basic building block right you will, in my experience, see a corresponding increase in business performance.

"Once you've delivered for staff they will deliver for you and it's not the other way around."

CSE NOT CSR

A successful business must in my view now look beyond the traditional ways of delivering value to shareholders and concentrate its focus on delivering for all stakeholders, that is to say, staff, customers, members, partners and, ultimately, society. It's incumbent on successful businesses globally to look at how its success can positively impact the communities around them and society as a whole. It must become the norm that great places to work produce exceptional business performance and that part of that success is used to improve society in a self-perpetuating cycle.

Happier employees create happier customers, and when customers understand what your business stands for, they will look for ways to do more business with you. This in turn will improve loyalty levels and ultimately strengthen your business. This core element must form part of your company's DNA and will reward you in different ways.

As it becomes part of the ethos and culture it impacts positively on staff retention, recruitment and engagement. For example, I once recruited a new member of staff who chose to join our company over a global firm. I believe that a large part of that decision was down to our evolving culture and ambition as a business. People will want to be part of it.

"It's about building long-term sustainable relationships with a wider stakeholder base, it's no longer about customers buying from you, it's about them buying into you."

Corporations must understand this, adapt quickly and fundamentally change their mind-set.

I have a problem with the phrase Corporate Social Responsibility (CSR) as I don't believe it goes far enough or is seen as a strategic part of business. I believe that being good is good for business. Apart from it being important for companies to give back, this must also be recognised as strategic in nature and demonstrate real engagement with all stakeholders. It's not simply about writing a cheque for a good cause; it's about engaging with that cause, that community and wider society as a whole, in a more dynamic and meaningful way. This is why in 2007, when I was working for an insurer in the UK, I coined the phrase Corporate Social Engagement or CSE to make up for, in my view, the shortcomings of the previous phrase and philosophy.

In the earlier part of my career I worked with a number of firms where I had to significantly transform businesses and turn them around. I guess that's essentially what I've done throughout my entire career, to fix things that needed attention and change. However, I began to consider whether there was a missing dimension here, a key element that could drive not just shareholder value but a wider stakeholder impact.

Later in 2007, I accepted another transformational role as

Managing Director back in Ireland having spent a number of years in England reshaping a business there. However, this time around I was intrigued by the company concerned.

This business was different in that all available profits it made went back to charities through a Trust which ultimately owned the entire business. This struck me as something pretty unique at the time, as the more successful the business was, the greater the ability of the organisation to give back.

I felt that this was a powerful model and one that could be used strategically to win business and attract and retain staff. I was immediately drawn to the business challenge and the principles of the company. I learned so much during my time there, and the business in Ireland grew from strength to strength during my tenure.

However, there was one aspect of the model I ultimately didn't understand. There was then a conscious and carefully managed policy of separating the core business strategy from its charitable distribution of profits and there didn't appear to be an obvious and strategic connection between both.

Whilst I completely respected the company's rationale, I felt that, given the right opportunity, I might get a chance to revisit this model and apply a different approach.

I once attended a leadership course in the excellent London Business School for a solid month, together with 22 other senior business leaders from around the world. It was an intense and rewarding programme but one particular day stood out for me.

We spent a day visiting Eastside Young Leader's Academy or EYLA in one of the toughest areas of London. When we arrived at this school we were greeted by the academy's founder, Ray Lewis, who had, in 2002, introduced a unique approach to social engagement based on the success of the model in Baton Rouge, Louisiana.

Not knowing what to expect, we were introduced to two teenage youths from the local community. Prompted by questions from our group, both youths began describing their businesses. They reluctantly and without eye contact described their margins, best market areas, best business days of the week, how they spot or recruit leaders. They spoke about how they promote them through the ranks rapidly, maintain discipline and co-ordinate distribution in what was a massively impressive model. Have you guessed the business yet? It was drugs.

Enter two similar youths in EYLA uniforms. These two individuals spoke with confidence about their own abilities and views, how they plan to contribute to the wider business and community world, even about their plans to attend Oxford College. Here's the catch, two years previously both EYLA students had been involved in the same business as the earlier two.

What had happened to create such a dramatic transformation in a short period of time? It was Ray Lewis and his amazing EYLA crew. To achieve this, they employ a unique and in some ways controversial approach. They set about identifying disruptive male youths in nearby schools and communities. They seek out individuals that have the ability to motivate others to follow their lead in terms of creating havoc within the system. Once identified, they first approach the individuals' mothers, as there is rarely a father around and these youngsters will tend to do what their mothers tell them. These strong male leaders are shown a different route to success through education with the EYLA. The academy only ever focuses on males, as they believe that if you can fix males in society then females tend to follow. Some will find this model to be controversial but in reality EYLA is changing the society around it by boldly identifying strong leaders with ability and giving them all the necessary educational tools to achieve amazing success. These leaders then act as a catalyst to encourage others to move away from a life of drugs and crime. This is societal change through the harnessing of hidden leadership abilities for monumental personal and cultural good.

This experience was probably the single greatest influence on my view that some of the stereotypical views and approaches we have engrained in our psyche needed to be challenged on a number of levels and corporates could, with direct engagement with communities, achieve significant societal change. I became determined that if ever I got a chance to transform another business as CEO

I would make sure that a key driver and measure of success would be societal impact, and that this impact would not only be good for communities but good for business. That opportunity arrived in August 2011.

After an initial few months settling into my new role as CEO, I duly presented a three-year business strategy to the Board in November 2011. As a 'Mutual' dating back to 1926, this company already had strong ideas around member value and mutuality. However, my presentation of the business strategy included a significant focus on CSE as a strategic driver that would deliver a stronger relationship with all stakeholders, engage staff in a new and innovative way, drive greater business performance and deliver significant difference to communities through societal change.

My initial proposal was to create a fund of €1m in five key strategic areas: Diaspora, Education, Community, Sport & Business Innovation.

Gaining Board support for the overall strategic plan is, of course, essential but introducing a fundamental shift in the mindset of a business is always going to be a challenge. This is especially true when it involves a significant financial spend and a radical cultural shift.

There was plenty of healthy challenge at this meeting around the concept of CSE and the Place, Business & Difference vision, but agreement was reached to move ahead with the entire plan. Creating this vision of a future organisation where CSE is seen as strategic as well as the right thing to do is always going to be a difficult form of rebirth for organisations. It is, as a result, crucial to the model's success that the CEO owns and believes 100% in this new model. Without the conviction of the CEO you will struggle to win Board approval and Stakeholder buy-in.

When I describe the PBD model and CSE approach to some organisations, I usually get the same response: "This is fantastic, Ronan, and it's amazing what your company is doing but it's easier to do this in a Mutual." And I usually give the same answer. This model for business applies to every business, whether it's a publicly quoted PLC,

Partnership or Mutual. This model drives a set of values that form the new DNA of your business which in turn creates a better culture for staff, improves performance, builds stronger stakeholder relationships, breathes new life into your brand and changes society in an extraordinary and measurable way. How can this not be seen as a positive thing by shareholders and the wider stakeholder base? If introduced in a genuine way so that it becomes an intrinsic part of the business, your organisation will rise in value internally as well as externally.

"Can you describe your company without mentioning what it does?"

I sometimes ask people to describe their company without mentioning what it does. In other words, if you work in an insurance company, describe what your company does without mentioning insurance.

If the individual pauses and struggles to describe their company, then we've a problem. You see, the modern company needs to be about much more than what it does. Don't get me wrong – it's important that you don't lose sight of the core activities of your business and that you ideally do it better than everyone else, but your company must stand for something more. It must have a personality, a character, a longer-term sustainability & value.

I believe that customers and employees are far more discerning than at any point in the past. They look beyond price to quickly seek to find out what your company stands for. Does it have principles? Does it respect the environment? Is it ethical? Does it care about staff and engage with the local community? Is it sustainable and does it make a difference to society?

This is the new currency, the measure of whether your business has a personality and whether it's something others will want to be around and engage with. Think about that for a moment, and if you can't describe your company beyond what it does, you need to change it now!

Your adoption of a CSE strategy must be for genuine reasons. Yes, it's important your company is recognised for the good it does and this, in turn, strengthens the profile of the company, but it must not be done purely for marketing reasons. Stakeholders will see through it immediately if so, and find it disingenuous. We are looking to build long-term value that will be sustainable so that all stakeholders buy into the total package and not just the product. If they trust the company they will want to engage with it and stick with it.

In 2012 Dublin Fire Brigade, a client, were celebrating their 150th Anniversary and a weekend of events around Dublin were planned. We received a call from them to see if we would sponsor some of the events and lend support. A meeting was set up and I posed a few questions about other sponsors and their involvement. It was explained that they had received fantastic support from Corporate Ireland and if we were interested in sponsoring the event they would ensure plenty of brand recognition and public profile. I asked them what was the most important aspect of the celebrations and was informed that a medal had being commissioned and would be presented to each individual fireman/woman at a ceremony on the first night of the celebrations. I asked who was sponsoring the cost of the medal and was informed that they couldn't get any corporate support here because there was no opportunity to brand the medal with a logo. This was simple for me and we agreed to cover the cost of producing the medal. They were blown away with this and invited me to speak on the night and present the medals. Unexpectedly, on the evening they also presented me with a medal and it sits proudly in my office to this day.

For me, this example really shows us that we need to rethink some of the norms in order to have deeper and more sustainable relationships with all stakeholders and create real legacy value.

It's what you do now that will inform whether future customers or employees will want to engage with you. It will be how you're measured and how you measure up.

CSE Framework

My introduction of a CSE Framework into the business operating model is based on a philosophy that corporates need to be more than responsible – they need to be accountable. This strategy allows you align your business and stakeholder profile to a systematic themed approach, giving back to society for social good.

The CSE Framework sets out the process of disbursing a Social Dividend. The entire framework is based on stakeholder's remit, which reflected in the six key strands. The funding programme is allied to pre-selected social categories relevant to your Stakeholder base.

Board of Directors

It's essential that the Board of Directors play a pivotal role in executing the CSE Framework in terms of not just agreeing the financial sign-off on a Social Dividend, but also the design, assessment and authorisation of same. There must be ownership of the framework from the top, and Directors must have a direct involvement in the consideration of individual projects or submissions of significant scale or importance.

This level of ownership instils a sense of appreciation of the wider benefits of the framework and creates a solid oversight, ensuring all activities and recommendations support the overarching aims of the firm and interests of all stakeholders. To facilitate this formally involves the establishment of a sub-committee of the Board, which should sit alongside other committees such as Audit, Risk, Nomination or Remuneration. The CSE Committee plays a key role in the overall framework.

CSE Committee

The CSE Committee is responsible for providing guidance and advice on the development of CSE initiatives in accordance with the CSE Framework. It should be chaired by a Board Director and membership should consist of a mix of executive and non-executive management to include the individuals responsible for the day-to-day running of CSE.

It should meet at least quarterly with formal reporting to the Board. It must have clear terms of reference and authority levels. The committee should consider and approve applications for funding submitted up to a certain threshold in terms of value or impact and provide recommendations to the Board.

Themes

Look for key themes that are important to your values as an organisation. Ensure they resonate with your staff, Board and stakeholders by completing detailed research and obtaining comprehensive feedback from all strands of your stakeholder base. Key to the success of the framework is to focus on developing no more than three key themes, rather than following the outdated and, in my view, flawed practice of aligning your company with a specific charity or charities. Agree themes that are important to your business in terms of strategy and beliefs and it will then be up to the sector to focus their approach or application for support based on your three key areas of interest, e.g. Education, Community, and Mental Health.

Partnerships

It's important to consider what your commitment as a company, in terms of issuing a Social Dividend and committing funds to certain themes, might leverage in terms of additional support. If, for example, you've agreed that education will be a key CSE theme for your organisation, start looking at other sector specific organisations, like-minded firms or government bodies who might be willing to match your initial contribution for a common cause.

In my experience, this approach has the potential to double or triple the size of the original investment and, as a result, reach a wider audience and achieve greater social impact. This association can also strengthen your own company's values, differentiate you from the pack and give your business a key strategic competitive edge as a result.

Action

It is critical to involve employees in the CSE Framework and to ensure that they have a say in how strategy is shaped and decisions are made. Don't fall into the trap of outsourcing the entire vetting process. Own it as an organisation. It's a core part of your business strategy and so why would you give one of the most important elements to another firm? In my experience, employees are incredibly willing to volunteer their own time to support CSE. Offer it out for staff to get involved and you'll be amazed at how genuinely interested, passionate and generous people can be.

In my case, staff worked after hours vetting applications, conducting formal interviews for larger submissions and ultimately making recommendations to the CSE Committee.

Impact

In order for the framework to be effective you must as a company ensure that you put in place a comprehensive set of practices to measure and report how effective your investment has been in terms of supporting the company's overall strategic direction.

It's essential to measure the overall impact of issuing a Social Dividend and to assess its success in real terms. Take the same time with CSE as you would with any other investment area and track its impact. Hard numbers are needed to assess and demonstrate to all stakeholders that this is money well spent, society has benefited and the business is stronger as a result. Formal reporting is a must and should be communicated regularly to all involved.

It's also important to build CSE goals into your company's overall key strategic objectives in order to focus everyone's mindset on building a sustainable business. CSE goals should also feature in employees development plans and form part of their formal appraisal review.

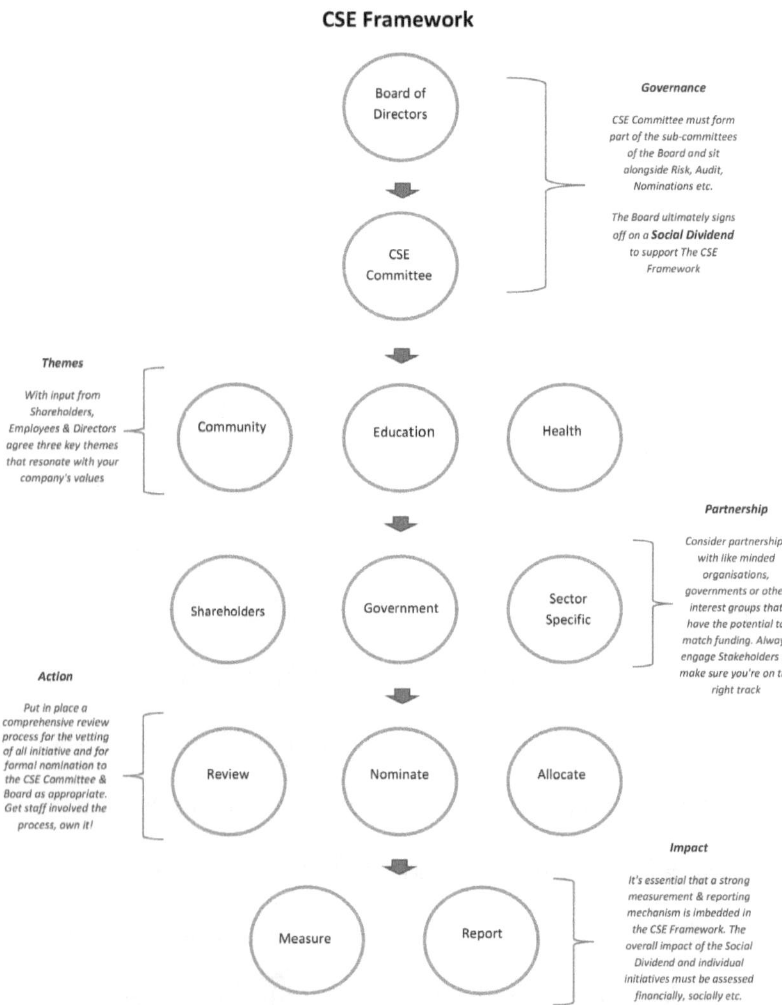

Is Your Annual Report A Good Read?

A key consideration when introducing a CSE Framework is how best to evidence and demonstrate its overall effectiveness to all stakeholders. In order to get this balance right, we began to consider how we could improve our Annual Report to reflect this. In 2012 we introduced another corporate first and produced a combined Stakeholder & Annual Report. This would include three clear sections: Stakeholder, Governance & Financial Reporting.

The goal here was to take a fresh look at annual reporting and to include a stakeholder section as an integral part of the report. I wanted a document where someone picking it up for the first time would actually want to read it and also get a sense of the wider reach of the company and it's culture.

I recall going out to dinner with my wife Annette one evening just after our AGM in 2012 and the release of our first Stakeholder & Annual Report. I was naturally very proud of the document and the incredible work that staff had put in to make it look so great. However, you're never quite sure whether you've hit the nail on the head until you receive feedback from someone completely unconnected with the business. Therefore, I was pleasantly surprised when we arrived home from our evening out to find our babysitter reading the report. I asked her what possessed her to pick it up and read it and her reply was, "I found it a very interesting read". I think when you find your babysitter reading your annual report you're definitely on the right track!

The Report was subsequently awarded The Annual Report of the Year 2013/2014 at the Irish Print Awards.

The Gathering

In considering CSE as a core strategy, it's important to examine how your funds might unlock additional or matching funds from other stakeholders or parties. I will give you an example.

One of the five themes we wanted to focus on was 'Diaspora' and the benefits it could bring to wider communities in Ireland.

In October 2012 I received a request for a meeting from Jim Miley who was heading up the Government's Gathering initiative for 2013, which was focused on reaching out to the Irish diaspora around the world and encouraging them to visit Ireland. I felt that this was a perfect fit for us and a proposal was agreed that would see the Irish Government match our initial amount, creating a joint fund of €2m.

The arrival of The Gathering in 2013 brought with it a

significant economic and social boost to communities, and everyone seemed involved in the many and varied events over the course of that year. It was officially the single biggest tourism event in the history of the State.

The initiative, a partnership between Local Authorities and the Government, was a perfect fit for our company, as it reached out to every community in Ireland through the local government network. Driven regionally through our members and the Local Authorities, the breadth and scale of the events targeting the Irish diaspora was unprecedented. As one of our five themed target-sectors for CSE, The Gathering reflected the sheer scale of the Irish diaspora, which was estimated at over 70 million people worldwide. The Gathering provided an added incentive for people with an ancestral link to Ireland to make 2013 the year they came to visit. One of the core objectives was to boost tourism numbers by bringing an additional 325,000 tourists into the country. The year-long celebration of festivals and events including Irish music, art, literature, dance, culture, heritage, sport, film and food, gave all the opportunity to look, with fresh eyes, at what our country had to offer. The Gathering reminded us of all the things that make Ireland great. Throughout 2013, Gathering events were held across the country, from bigger and better St. Patrick's Day celebrations and summer festivals to school and family reunions and dances in the local sports hall. The success of the project is a story of community spirit and the drive of people to get involved.

When you deal directly with people and communities, you empower them to go out and do things, to just get on with it. This funding must go to the core and not into a bureaucratic machine that may suck the living daylights out of the entire initiative. I believe some large well-established companies sat on the fence for too long in respect of The Gathering, wondering what it would do for them, what it could deliver for their business. This was never about brand leverage or The Gathering working for Corporate Ireland; it was about motivating communities to get involved, to create events, to bring people home and generate jobs and income for local towns and villages across the country.

The recognition that we as a company received for this support was incredible and the evidence of making a difference was clearly felt around Ireland. It also had a very positive impact on our own staff, members and wider stakeholder base. It drew us all much closer together and I felt strongly that this recipe should, given the right opportunity, be repeated again in other areas.

It can be difficult sometimes to measure the exact impact of a specific initiative but we completed an evaluation of our support alone and established that it had delivered 84,960 additional visitors and generated an estimated €50m to the Irish economy.

THE MIDDLE LINE

"The provision of the €1 million by your company was

a welcome boost and addressed an important gap in The

Gathering events programme and funding needs

at county level.

Similarly, The Gathering Community Events Fund, financed

from The Gathering budget and administered by local

authorities, provided an innovative and flexible solution to

the micro funding requirements of local and

community events."

The Gathering Final Report, December 2013,

Fáilte Ireland

Another important aspect of this initiative was the way in which public and private partnerships can work together. If you have a specific CSE theme you want to focus on, try and identify an initiative that already exists at government level or could be created as part of an overall joint effort. Identify an initiative that fits a common objective and creates a positive difference to society, ask others to match your funding and see if you can double or treble the fund as a result. It's an approach that worked well for me and one I replicated with other initiatives following the success of The Gathering.

A New Age Of Corporate Philanthropy

"My vision for the future is a society supported by local business where corporates see it as an absolute necessity for their future long-term success to have a clearly defined CSE strategy, issue an Annual Social Dividend and deliver a stronger business and society as a result."

I believe that future philanthropists will emerge from the corporate world. The amount of individual personal wealth has taken a hit in recent years and, whilst there are signs of a global recovery, it may never reach the same heights as before. Corporate rather than personal philanthropy is emerging at great pace and this is where I believe those seeking support should focus.

There are businesses led by individuals with a limited

personal wealth but running successful companies. As the Social Dividend model emerges over the next 5-10 years, organisations will need to adopt a mindset that incorporates a strong sense of being good because it's the right thing to do, and that it will improve their company's performance. Charities and fundraisers will need to focus on companies that adopt this new model and focus on aligning their strategies collectively to create initiatives that serve the wider community and which are directly related to a company's values and long-term strategic goals.

This new model will see fewer companies aligning themselves to specific charity organisations but focussing on legacy-type projects that directly impact society and add value to their business. They will, in turn, identify areas they wish to focus on and target opportunities that mirror their objectives.

In 2013 we repeated this formula and created a new €1m fund to support local communities around Ireland. The Community Fund was designed to specifically target the smaller local and voluntary groups in villages and towns throughout the country to promote social inclusion through the stimulation and support of local organisations and initiatives.

The Fund was open to all local community and voluntary groups, clubs or associations as well as not-for-profit and charitable organisations operating at a local level within Ireland. Applications were categorised under six specific activities: Arts and Culture, Community Development, Environment, Elderly, Physical Activity & Sport and Youth. Organisations were invited to apply for funding of between €2,500–€7,000 or €10,000–€15,000, depending on their needs. We chose to allocate the fund in this way for two reasons.

Firstly, by keeping the amount of individual funding awards relatively low, we knew we would be able to support a large and diverse range of applications.

Secondly, we knew that it had been harder than ever for smaller local community and voluntary groups to raise funds in recent years. We also knew that a relatively small lump sum could make all the difference.

Using an on-line application tool, we made the process readily accessible and submissions could be completed quickly and conveniently anywhere. An incredible 1,987 applications were received for the €1m Community Fund and it was the third large-scale initiative to be launched under the company's CSE Framework. Applications had steadily come in over the application period but there was a major surge in the number of applications in the last couple of days before the Fund closed to applications at 5 p.m. on Friday 17 January. Applications were received from a huge variety of organisations for all kinds of projects from almost every town and county in the country.

This surge in applications just before the closing deadline caught us by surprise and created a challenge in terms of evaluating submissions. In a move which, for me, really emphasises the CSE philosophy, over 30 members of staff volunteered to give up their personal time to complete these evaluations. This brought the values and culture we were seeking to promote within the company to a whole new level. The message is clear: if you want your staff to live and breathe your company's values then get them directly involved in deciding what these values are and fully engaged in how they're rolled out.

I was pleasantly surprised and proud to read the following coverage in the national press:

"As one door opened on Friday at noon, another closed five hours later. IPB put aside €1m and invited community and voluntary groups to make a submission for a share of this money. In stark contrast to what happened at the CRC, this is an extraordinary venture for a company to undertake. IPB says it sees this as a social dividend, reaching right down into the heart of communities where there are plenty of willing volunteers but very little money. The idea is to help groups get projects off the ground – a small bit of money can make a big difference. Grants of up to €10,000 will be made which IPB hopes will get worthy projects started.

IPB, which late last year also pledged €50,000 to help the FAI (Football Association of Ireland) expand its ground-breaking

Late Night League programme, opted not to shout from the rooftops about this fund – choosing instead to communicate directly with groups via Local Authorities and other outlets – and yet when Friday's p.m. deadline expired, an incredible 1,987 submissions had been lodged by community groups."

Sunday Independent, 19 January 2014

LATE NIGHT LEAGUES

I was asked to speak at the launch of the Federation of Irish Sport Insurance Scheme launch in Dec 2012 and in preparation for my address I started to look at the social impact that sport has in communities.

I recalled my time living in England for a few years in the beautiful country village of Cliddesden on the outskirts of Basingstoke and trying to decipher the difference between what brought communities together when compared to Ireland. It appeared to me that it was the Church in England that acted as the catalyst but back home it was sport, and particularly the Gaelic Athletic Association (GAA).

In looking for raw examples of where sport had a measurable impact on society I came across The Late Night Leagues (LNL) programme. It's a unique and innovative approach to tackling the problem of anti-social behaviour, run by the FAI in partnership with Dublin's four Local Authorities since 2008. The programme had been incredibly successful in Dublin with 1,100 young footballers taking part in 2013.

One statistic that stood out for me and one I referenced in my address was research that suggested Garda (police) sub-divisions that deploy the LNL programme had seen a 26% reduction in anti-social related calls into local stations versus sub-divisions where LNL weren't deployed.

We decided to get behind this initiative and roll it out nationally to the benefit of communities nationwide. This involved a commitment of €50,000 in terms of funding and a close working partnership with the FAI, Local Authorities and An Garda Síochána (Irish Police Force).

The aim of the LNL programme is to encourage at-risk young people from disadvantaged areas to participate in meaningful activities at times deemed to be prime anti-social hours, thereby reducing levels of anti-social behaviour. The programme was initially aimed at young people in the 16-19 year-old age bracket and was so successful that it has since grown to encompass 12-15 year-olds as well. The programme and its positive effect was noticed by community Gardaí and in 2010 the Garda Assistant Commissioner for the Dublin Region formally announced that An Garda Síochána would be becoming an official partner of the LNL programme. As well as giving the youths involved a focus for their evenings, the involvement of the Gardaí in the programme has meant they also gain a better understanding of, and respect for, the role of the Gardaí in their local communities.

The LNL operates during winter months when teenagers have few other social options. In 2013 the programme catered for 1,100 young footballers from 19 centres around Dublin, all in areas deemed to be disadvantaged. The competition drew to an exciting close at the finals which were played in Irishtown Stadium on Friday, 6 December 2013. 450 young people took part in games across 10 pitches and the stands were packed as local communities turned out in force to cheer on their teams. The atmosphere created on that night alone was proof of the huge impact the LNL programme was having.

The roll-out began in March 2014 with Late Night Leagues being established in a minimum of 32 centres across the country.

Makes You Want To Work Harder!

One of the other areas we focused on was education, and, particularly, access for those who might never have had the opportunity of third-level education. We already had a strong and pioneering relationship in place with Dublin City University (DCU) but had begun to work with Limerick Institute of Technology (LIT).

I'd first met then LIT President, Maria Hinfelaar, at a function in Cork and over dinner she described, in an incredibly real and passionate way, the challenges LIT faced in not just providing access to education but in encouraging students to stick with their studies in year two and year three. The drop-out rate had reached over 40% during the height of the financial crisis.

Working with Maria and her team, we put a scholarship in

place to help assist them with this challenge and launched our first bursary later in 2013.

I was delighted to be invited by Maria to present the first five scholarships and say a few words at the college later that year. Travelling down to Limerick that day, I recall being driven by my colleague so that I could essentially work during the two-hour trip. It was a crucial time for the business as we were in the middle of a strategic acquisition. It would have been easy, given this, for me to delegate the trip to LIT to someone else and for me to focus my time on the acquisition, but that would have been the wrong decision.

I met the five scholarship winners and their families when I arrived and was immediately struck by the enormity of the occasion. In awe, I listened to two of the recipients speak publicly for their first time about how much these scholarships meant to them and their families, about how they were the first in their families ever to attend college and how this was the single biggest opportunity they'd ever had.

I remember getting back to the car after the ceremony and, before starting our journey back to Dublin, saying to my colleague, "You think you're busy, you think you can't afford the time to make trips likes this and that someone else can do it. But then you experience first-hand the tangible difference companies can make and it just makes you want to work harder."

I suppose my point is that, as a leader, you must witness the impact yourself to receive the assurance that your company's success is delivering real social change and at the same time motivating your staff to work harder than ever. In short, everybody wins!

New Old Model

If you look back in time, you'll notice that before communities started looking for support from governments for funding to develop their communities, local businesses were the first to step in. In one sense, the model I am proposing is very similar.

It's about successful businesses working with communities in a deliberate and engaging way to support an individual, community, village, town, city or country.

This corporate social engagement model, if carefully designed and genuinely applied, will not only act as a force for good but also enhance every aspect of your business in a perpetual cycle of success for everyone that chooses to engage. In my experience, it will create an eagerness to engage with your business in a social and commercial way like never before.

I recall tendering for a significant piece of new business. As a local Irish business, we were up against some much larger global companies. After a competitive process, we, along with a small number of other finalists, were asked to present directly to the client as the last part of the tender programme. I attended the presentation together with two other colleagues and we split the presentation three ways. The prospective client, a very large business, quizzed us about all the usual business stuff but decided to concentrate on our Social Dividend, CSE Framework and culture of the business. We ultimately won the account without being the most competitive and later learned that the client found great synergy with our company's values and CSE approach.

Competitive advantage in business is changing and if you are not reshaping your organisation's strategy to include an emphasis on creating a positive impact on society, declaring a social dividend and engaging with all your stakeholders in a genuine way, you will lose out!

Do It Now

I would urge you and your company to start looking at introducing a CSE Framework and making it an intrinsic part of your future strategic direction. I would also urge you to think seriously about committing to a Social Dividend structure when annual financial performance allows it. Focus on getting the 'Place' right for your teams and in turn the 'Business' will prosper and help create a platform to introduce a 'Difference' to the communities around you.

"This is the new model for business and focusing on these elements will strengthen your Top, Bottom and Middle-Line!"

In my experience, this new model for business will transform your company and create a new DNA that staff, customers and society will be proud to be associated with. It has, in my time at the helm, produced the best results in terms of Place, Business & Difference.

It's now time for a new challenge and to change the way business is done on the global stage. Here we go!

About the Author

Ronan Foley is an experienced CEO with a strong track record of successfully transforming businesses and making change happen.

His leadership has delivered profitable growth for every company he has led and, in his most recent tenure as CEO, the company recorded the best financial results in its 90-year history.

He has been named one of Ireland's top 100 CEOs and listed as a Global 100 Irish CEO by *Business & Finance*, noting 'strong leadership attributes and leading companies through innovation, expansion and growth'. He was announced as 'Businessman of the Year' in 2014 by Chambers Ireland, citing his 'commercial achievements, particularly in transforming and growing businesses and for innovative thought-leadership in the area of next generation business strategy and CSR'.

His innovation led his last company to be the first in corporate history to introduce a Social Dividend as part of its formal annual reporting and his commitment to transparency by introducing the first ever combined Stakeholder and Annual Report in an Irish context are examples of his achievements in business and corporate citizenship.

He believes that 'being good is also good for business' and is passionate about building sustainable businesses that focus on meeting and exceeding the needs of all stakeholders.

Ronan lives in Dublin, Ireland with his wife, Annette, and two daughters, Mia & Siân.

You can find him at www.ronanfoley.com.